JAN 1 5

JR. GRAPHIC AMERICAN LEGENDS

MOLLY BROWN

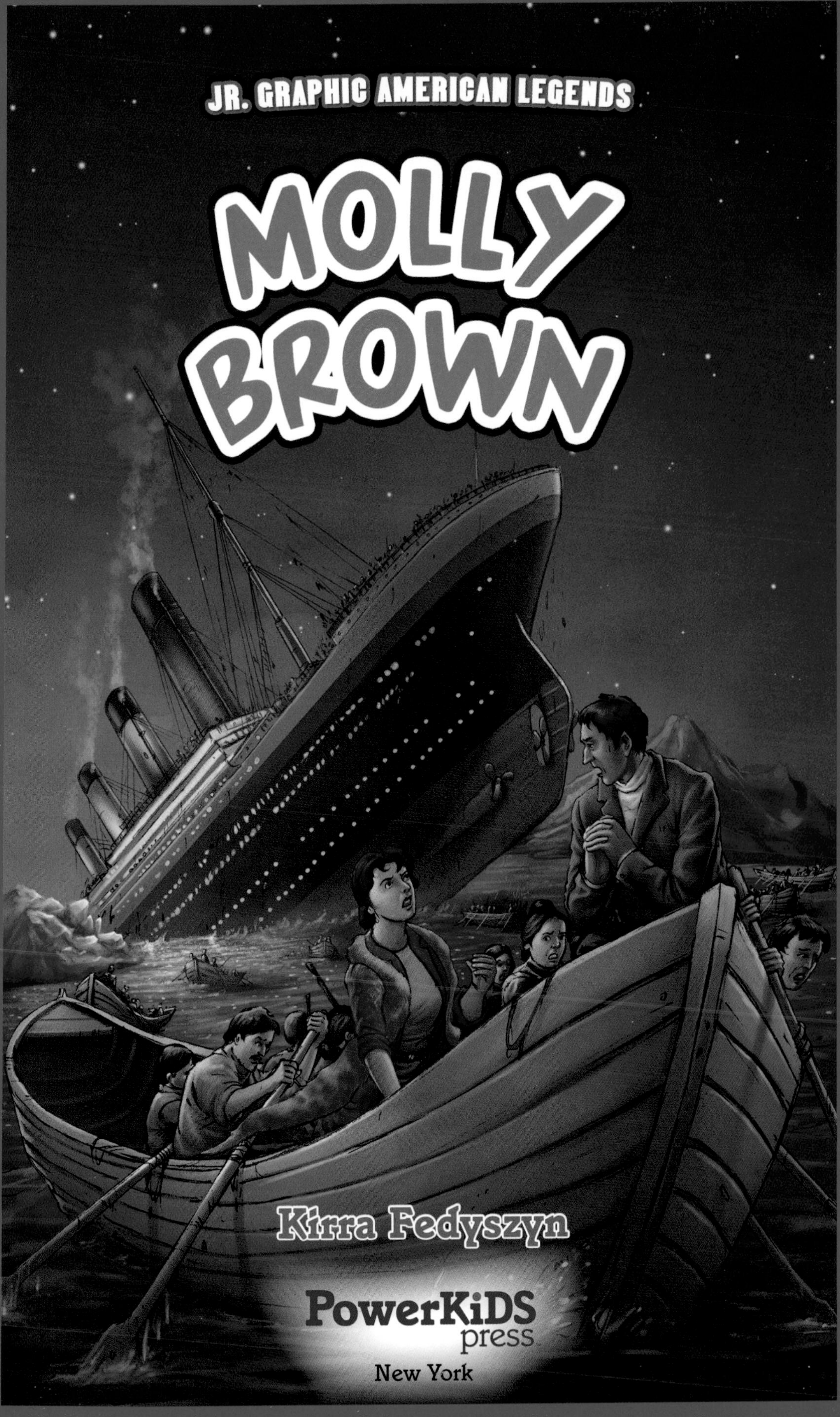

Kirra Fedyszyn

PowerKiDS press

New York

Published in 2015 by The Rosen Publishing Group, Inc.
29 East 21st Street, New York, NY 10010

First Edition

Editor: Joanne Randolph
Book Design: Contentra Technologies
Illustrations: Contentra Technologies

Library of Congress Cataloging-in-Publication Data

Fedyszyn, Kirra.
Molly Brown / by Kirra Fedyszyn. — First edition.
    pages cm. — (Jr. graphic American legends)
Includes index.
ISBN 978-1-4777-7202-7 (library binding) — ISBN 978-1-4777-7201-0 (pbk.) — ISBN 978-1-4777-7203-4 (6-pack)
1. Brown, Margaret Tobin, 1867-1932—Comic books, strips, etc. 2. Brown, Margaret Tobin, 1867-1932—Juvenile literature. 3. Titanic (Steamship)—Comic books, strips, etc. 4. Titanic (Steamship)—Juvenile literature. 5. Women social reformers—United States—Biography—Comic books, strips, etc. 6. Women social reformers—United States—Biography—Juvenile literature. 7. Social reformers—United States—Biography—Comic books, strips, etc. 8. Social reformers—United States—Biography—Juvenile literature. 9. Graphic novels. I. Title.
CT275.B7656F44 2015
303.48'4092—dc23
                                      2013050446

Manufactured in the United States of America
CPSIA Compliance Information: Batch #WS14PK2: For Further Information contact Rosen Publishing, New York, New York at 1-800-237-9932

Contents

Introduction

In 1912, the RMS *Titanic* was the largest ship ever to sail the ocean. It left on its very first **voyage**, from England to the United States, on April 10. Four days later, though, **disaster** struck when the ship hit an iceberg and began to sink. As the ship went down, one female passenger helped others into **lifeboats** before taking command of a lifeboat herself. Once they were rescued, she continued to help the survivors, making sure everyone was taken care of. We know this woman as Molly Brown, though her real name was Margaret. Not only did Margaret become a hero on the *Titanic*, she also used her wealth and connections to fight for the rights of women and children.

Main Characters

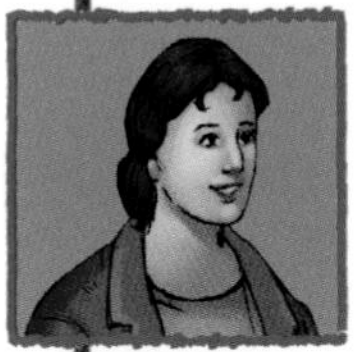

Margaret Tobin Brown (1867–1932) The daughter of Irish **immigrants**, Margaret's life had humble beginnings. After her husband worked his way up from miner to **superintendent** and found a new way to mine gold, she became a wealthy member of Denver society. She fought for human rights and education, but she is best known for her actions during and after the sinking of the *Titanic*.

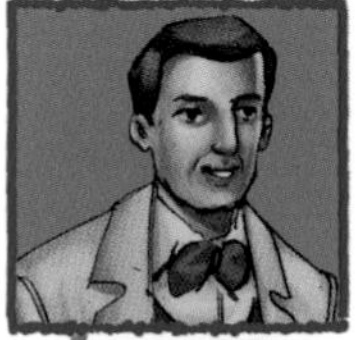

James Joseph Brown (1854–1922) Margaret's husband. He was a mining **engineer** and rose through the ranks until he was in charge of the mine where he worked. He later found a way to mine gold that had been impossible to reach, bringing great wealth to his family.

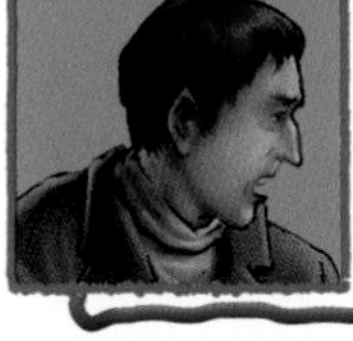

Robert Hichens (1882–1940) A crew member on the *Titanic*. He was in the same lifeboat as Margaret. As the ship was going down, he insisted that they row away quickly rather than try to rescue other passengers, even though their lifeboat was less than half full.

MOLLY BROWN

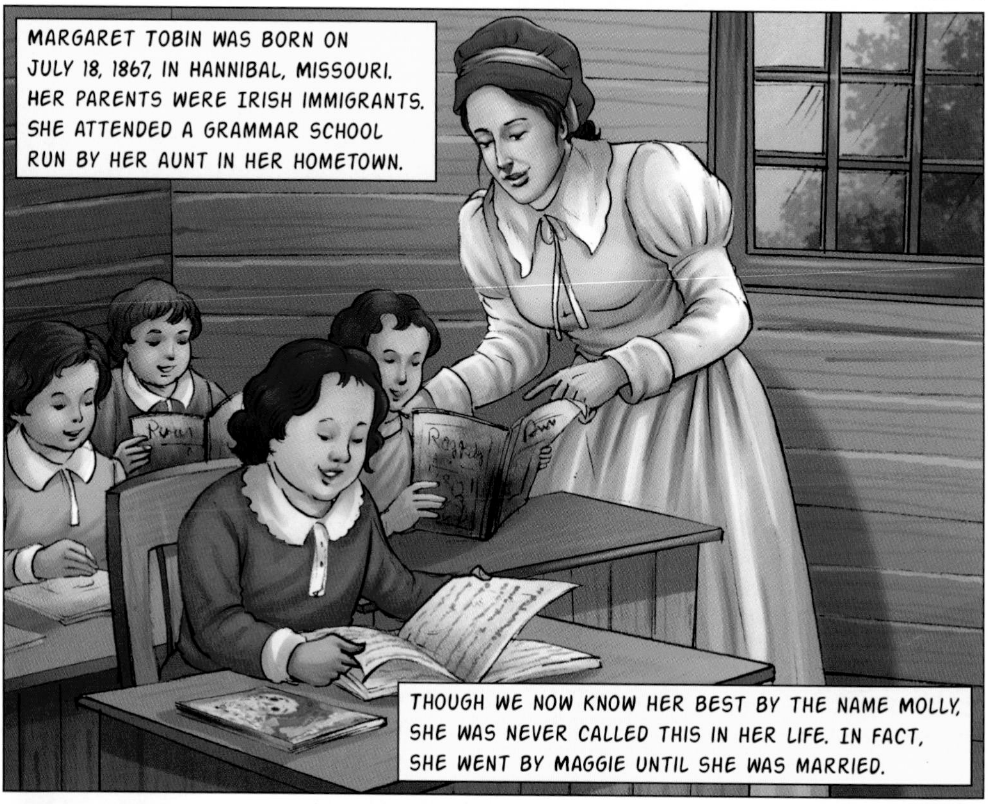
MARGARET TOBIN WAS BORN ON JULY 18, 1867, IN HANNIBAL, MISSOURI. HER PARENTS WERE IRISH IMMIGRANTS. SHE ATTENDED A GRAMMAR SCHOOL RUN BY HER AUNT IN HER HOMETOWN.
THOUGH WE NOW KNOW HER BEST BY THE NAME MOLLY, SHE WAS NEVER CALLED THIS IN HER LIFE. IN FACT, SHE WENT BY MAGGIE UNTIL SHE WAS MARRIED.

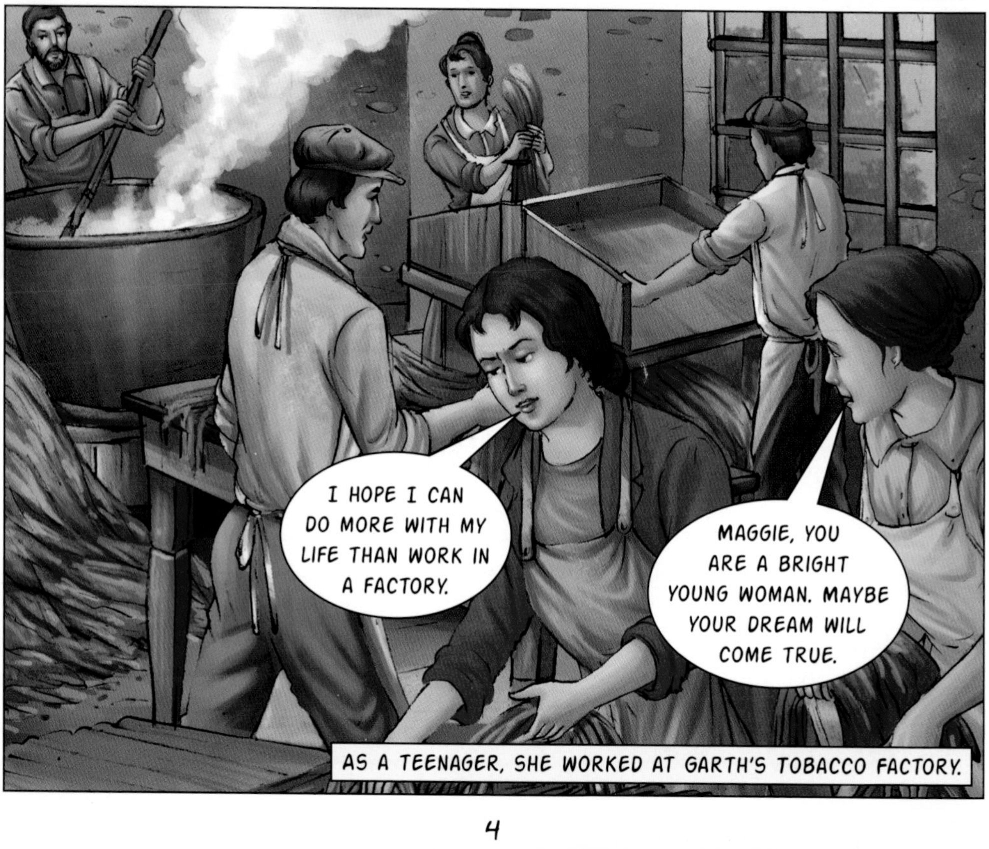
I HOPE I CAN DO MORE WITH MY LIFE THAN WORK IN A FACTORY.
MAGGIE, YOU ARE A BRIGHT YOUNG WOMAN. MAYBE YOUR DREAM WILL COME TRUE.
AS A TEENAGER, SHE WORKED AT GARTH'S TOBACCO FACTORY.

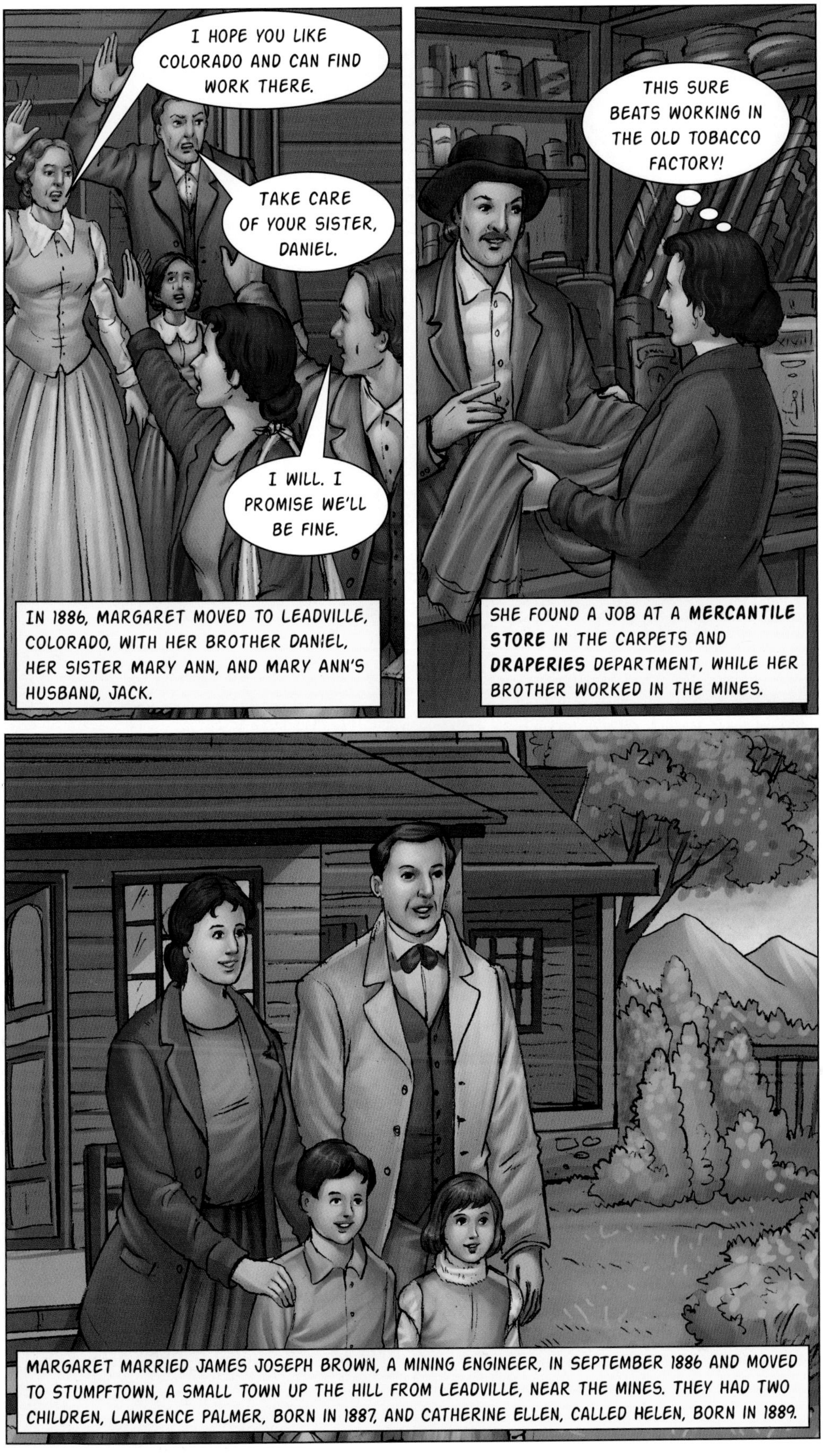
I HOPE YOU LIKE COLORADO AND CAN FIND WORK THERE.
TAKE CARE OF YOUR SISTER, DANIEL.
I WILL. I PROMISE WE'LL BE FINE.
IN 1886, MARGARET MOVED TO LEADVILLE, COLORADO, WITH HER BROTHER DANIEL, HER SISTER MARY ANN, AND MARY ANN'S HUSBAND, JACK.
THIS SURE BEATS WORKING IN THE OLD TOBACCO FACTORY!
SHE FOUND A JOB AT A **MERCANTILE STORE** IN THE CARPETS AND **DRAPERIES** DEPARTMENT, WHILE HER BROTHER WORKED IN THE MINES.
MARGARET MARRIED JAMES JOSEPH BROWN, A MINING ENGINEER, IN SEPTEMBER 1886 AND MOVED TO STUMPFTOWN, A SMALL TOWN UP THE HILL FROM LEADVILLE, NEAR THE MINES. THEY HAD TWO CHILDREN, LAWRENCE PALMER, BORN IN 1887, AND CATHERINE ELLEN, CALLED HELEN, BORN IN 1889.

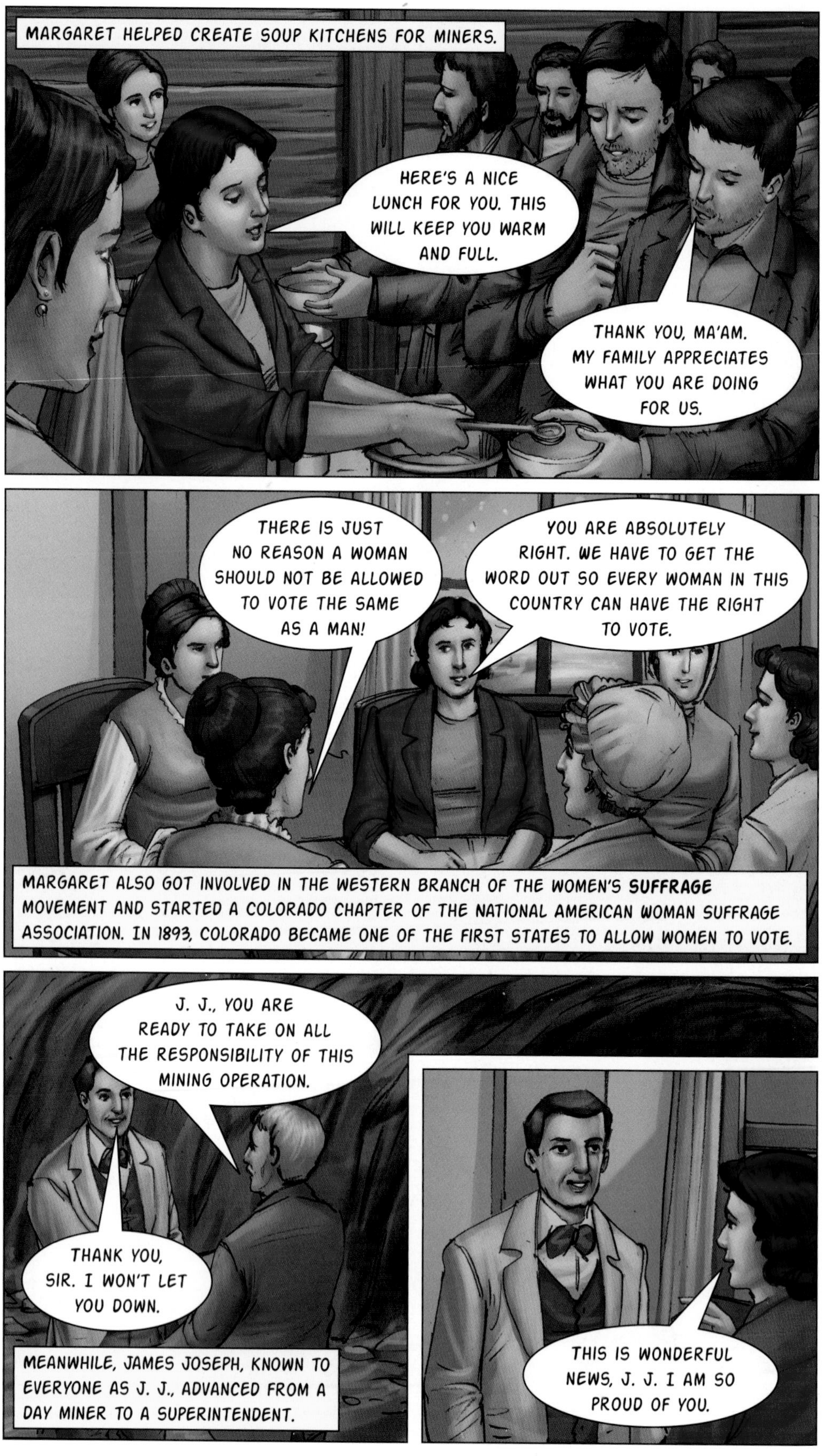
MARGARET HELPED CREATE SOUP KITCHENS FOR MINERS.
HERE'S A NICE LUNCH FOR YOU. THIS WILL KEEP YOU WARM AND FULL.
THANK YOU, MA'AM. MY FAMILY APPRECIATES WHAT YOU ARE DOING FOR US.
THERE IS JUST NO REASON A WOMAN SHOULD NOT BE ALLOWED TO VOTE THE SAME AS A MAN!
YOU ARE ABSOLUTELY RIGHT. WE HAVE TO GET THE WORD OUT SO EVERY WOMAN IN THIS COUNTRY CAN HAVE THE RIGHT TO VOTE.
MARGARET ALSO GOT INVOLVED IN THE WESTERN BRANCH OF THE WOMEN'S **SUFFRAGE** MOVEMENT AND STARTED A COLORADO CHAPTER OF THE NATIONAL AMERICAN WOMAN SUFFRAGE ASSOCIATION. IN 1893, COLORADO BECAME ONE OF THE FIRST STATES TO ALLOW WOMEN TO VOTE.
J. J., YOU ARE READY TO TAKE ON ALL THE RESPONSIBILITY OF THIS MINING OPERATION.
THANK YOU, SIR. I WON'T LET YOU DOWN.
MEANWHILE, JAMES JOSEPH, KNOWN TO EVERYONE AS J. J., ADVANCED FROM A DAY MINER TO A SUPERINTENDENT.
THIS IS WONDERFUL NEWS, J. J. I AM SO PROUD OF YOU.

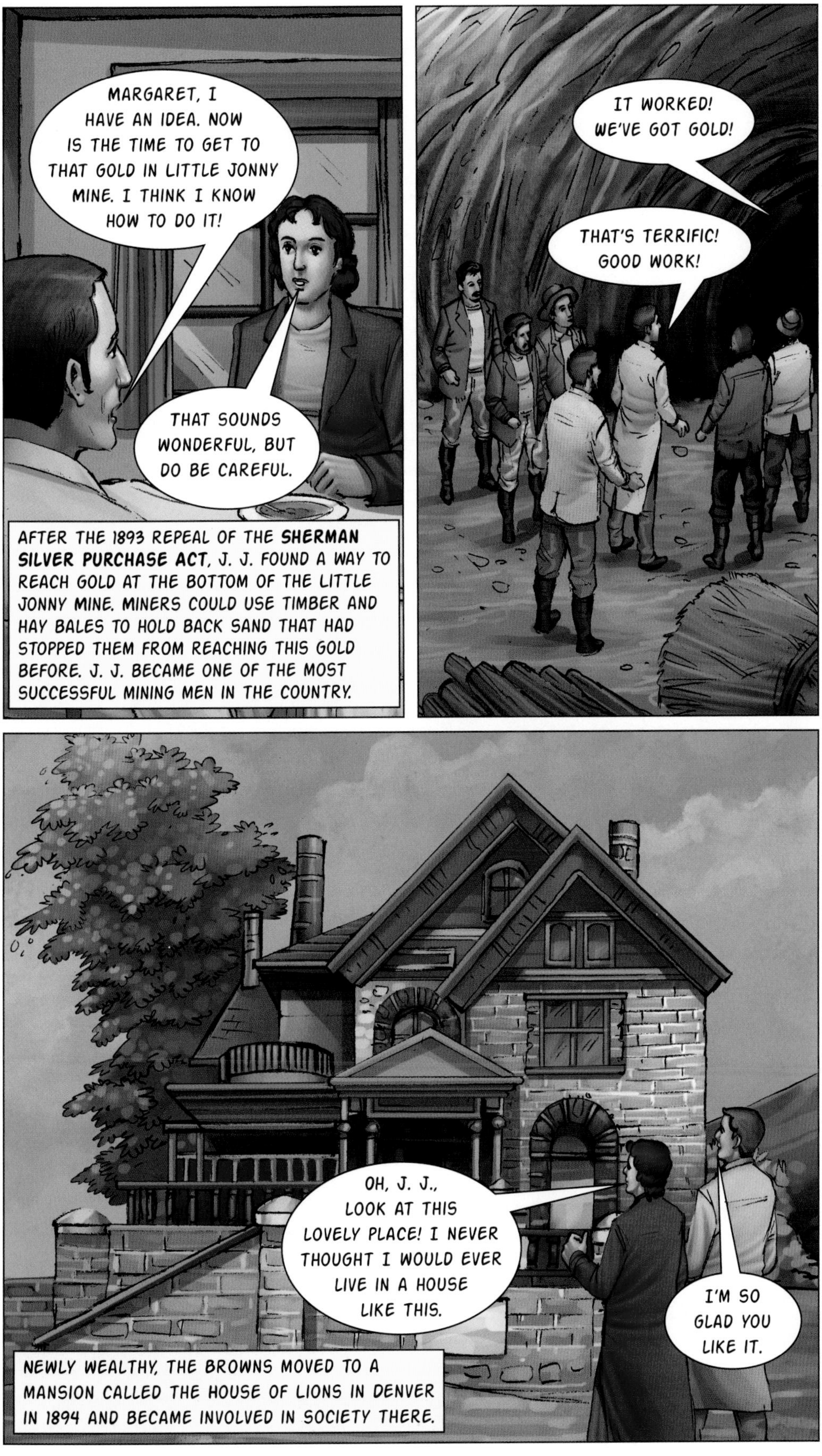
MARGARET, I HAVE AN IDEA. NOW IS THE TIME TO GET TO THAT GOLD IN LITTLE JONNY MINE. I THINK I KNOW HOW TO DO IT!
THAT SOUNDS WONDERFUL, BUT DO BE CAREFUL.
AFTER THE 1893 REPEAL OF THE SHERMAN SILVER PURCHASE ACT, J. J. FOUND A WAY TO REACH GOLD AT THE BOTTOM OF THE LITTLE JONNY MINE. MINERS COULD USE TIMBER AND HAY BALES TO HOLD BACK SAND THAT HAD STOPPED THEM FROM REACHING THIS GOLD BEFORE. J. J. BECAME ONE OF THE MOST SUCCESSFUL MINING MEN IN THE COUNTRY.
IT WORKED! WE'VE GOT GOLD!
THAT'S TERRIFIC! GOOD WORK!
OH, J. J., LOOK AT THIS LOVELY PLACE! I NEVER THOUGHT I WOULD EVER LIVE IN A HOUSE LIKE THIS.
I'M SO GLAD YOU LIKE IT.
NEWLY WEALTHY, THE BROWNS MOVED TO A MANSION CALLED THE HOUSE OF LIONS IN DENVER IN 1894 AND BECAME INVOLVED IN SOCIETY THERE.

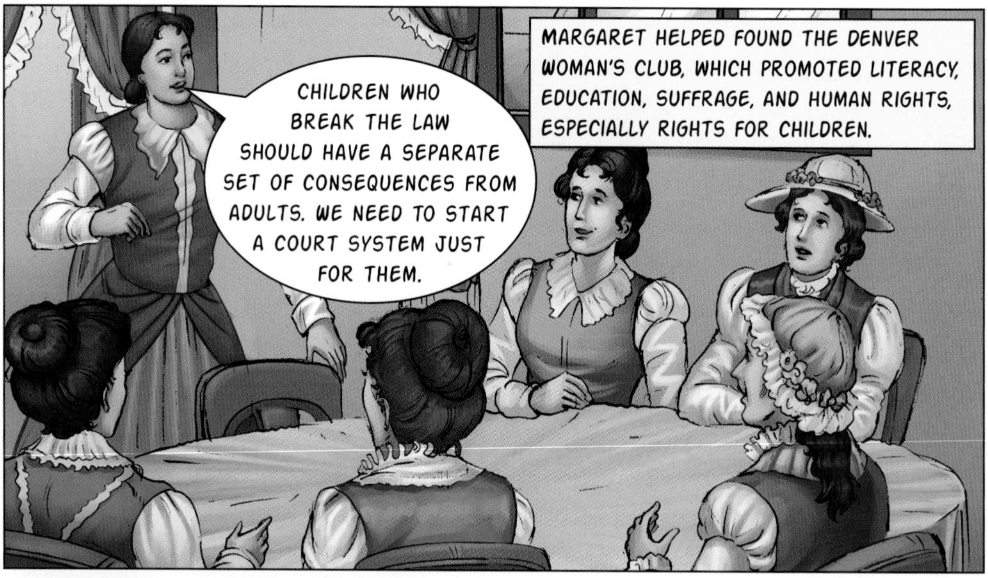
MARGARET HELPED FOUND THE DENVER WOMAN'S CLUB, WHICH PROMOTED LITERACY, EDUCATION, SUFFRAGE, AND HUMAN RIGHTS, ESPECIALLY RIGHTS FOR CHILDREN.
CHILDREN WHO BREAK THE LAW SHOULD HAVE A SEPARATE SET OF CONSEQUENCES FROM ADULTS. WE NEED TO START A COURT SYSTEM JUST FOR THEM.

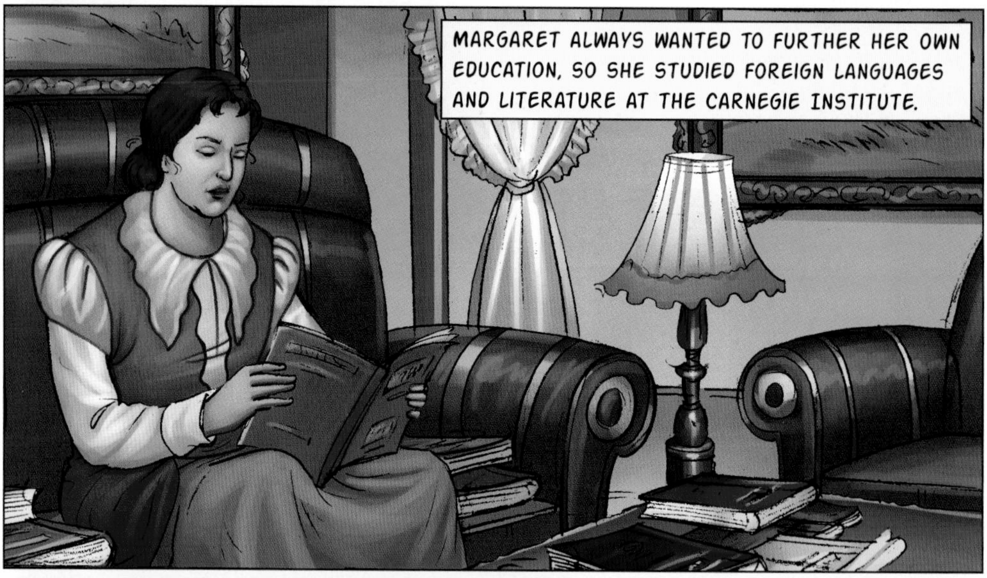
MARGARET ALWAYS WANTED TO FURTHER HER OWN EDUCATION, SO SHE STUDIED FOREIGN LANGUAGES AND LITERATURE AT THE CARNEGIE INSTITUTE.

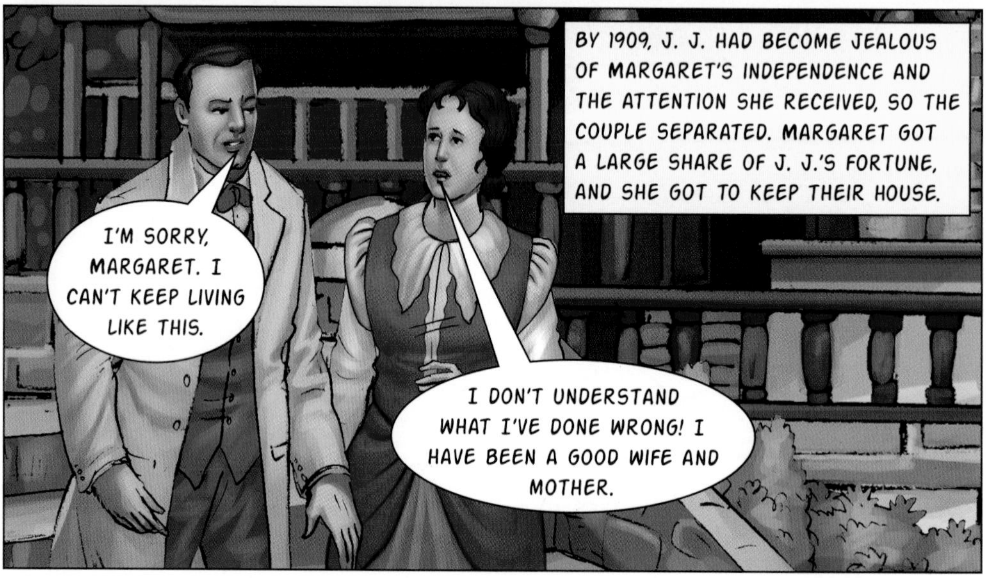
BY 1909, J. J. HAD BECOME JEALOUS OF MARGARET'S INDEPENDENCE AND THE ATTENTION SHE RECEIVED, SO THE COUPLE SEPARATED. MARGARET GOT A LARGE SHARE OF J. J.'S FORTUNE, AND SHE GOT TO KEEP THEIR HOUSE.
I'M SORRY, MARGARET. I CAN'T KEEP LIVING LIKE THIS.
I DON'T UNDERSTAND WHAT I'VE DONE WRONG! I HAVE BEEN A GOOD WIFE AND MOTHER.

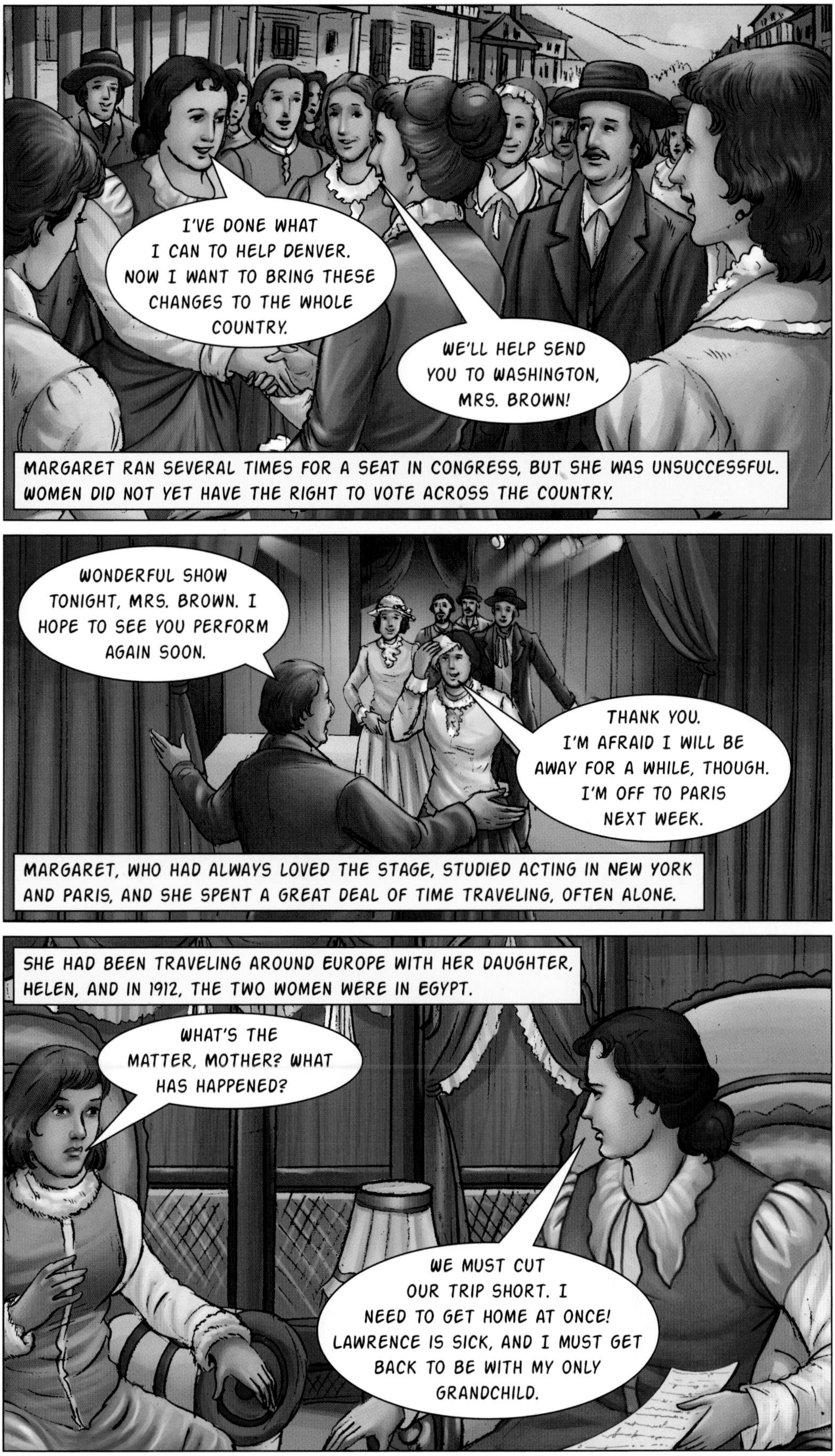
I'VE DONE WHAT I CAN TO HELP DENVER. NOW I WANT TO BRING THESE CHANGES TO THE WHOLE COUNTRY.
WE'LL HELP SEND YOU TO WASHINGTON, MRS. BROWN!
MARGARET RAN SEVERAL TIMES FOR A SEAT IN CONGRESS, BUT SHE WAS UNSUCCESSFUL. WOMEN DID NOT YET HAVE THE RIGHT TO VOTE ACROSS THE COUNTRY.
WONDERFUL SHOW TONIGHT, MRS. BROWN. I HOPE TO SEE YOU PERFORM AGAIN SOON.
THANK YOU. I'M AFRAID I WILL BE AWAY FOR A WHILE, THOUGH. I'M OFF TO PARIS NEXT WEEK.
MARGARET, WHO HAD ALWAYS LOVED THE STAGE, STUDIED ACTING IN NEW YORK AND PARIS, AND SHE SPENT A GREAT DEAL OF TIME TRAVELING, OFTEN ALONE.
SHE HAD BEEN TRAVELING AROUND EUROPE WITH HER DAUGHTER, HELEN, AND IN 1912, THE TWO WOMEN WERE IN EGYPT.
WHAT'S THE MATTER, MOTHER? WHAT HAS HAPPENED?
WE MUST CUT OUR TRIP SHORT. I NEED TO GET HOME AT ONCE! LAWRENCE IS SICK, AND I MUST GET BACK TO BE WITH MY ONLY GRANDCHILD.

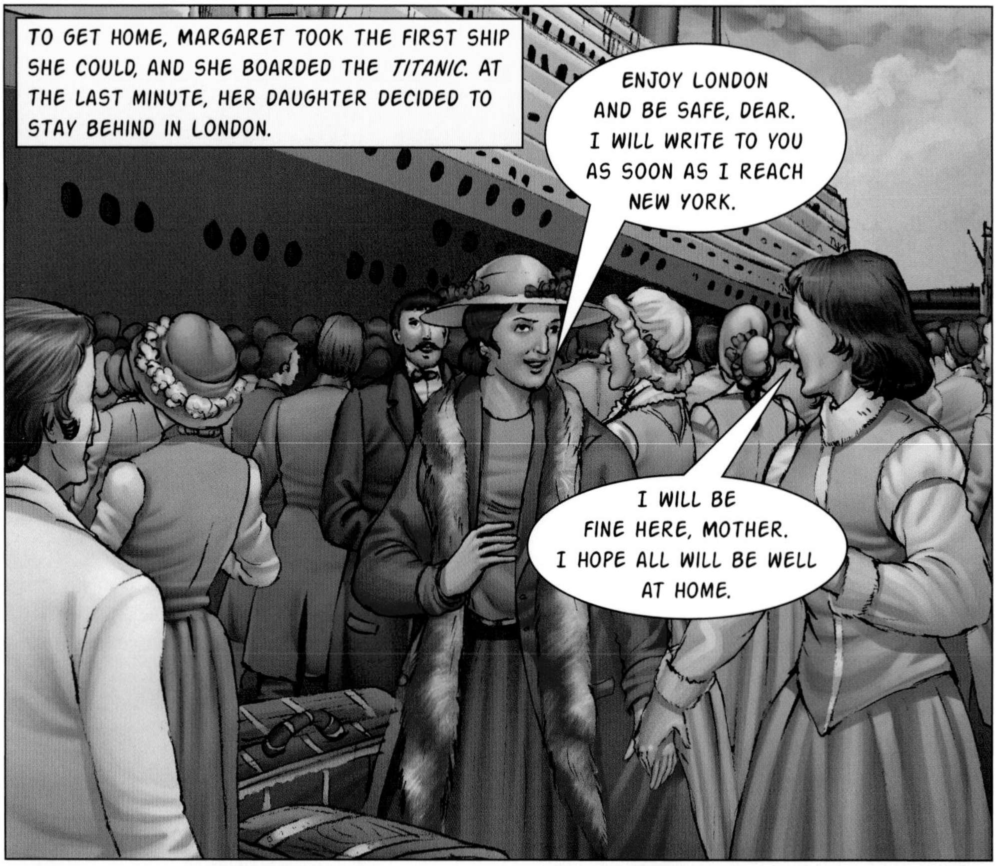
TO GET HOME, MARGARET TOOK THE FIRST SHIP SHE COULD, AND SHE BOARDED THE *TITANIC*. AT THE LAST MINUTE, HER DAUGHTER DECIDED TO STAY BEHIND IN LONDON.
ENJOY LONDON AND BE SAFE, DEAR. I WILL WRITE TO YOU AS SOON AS I REACH NEW YORK.
I WILL BE FINE HERE, MOTHER. I HOPE ALL WILL BE WELL AT HOME.

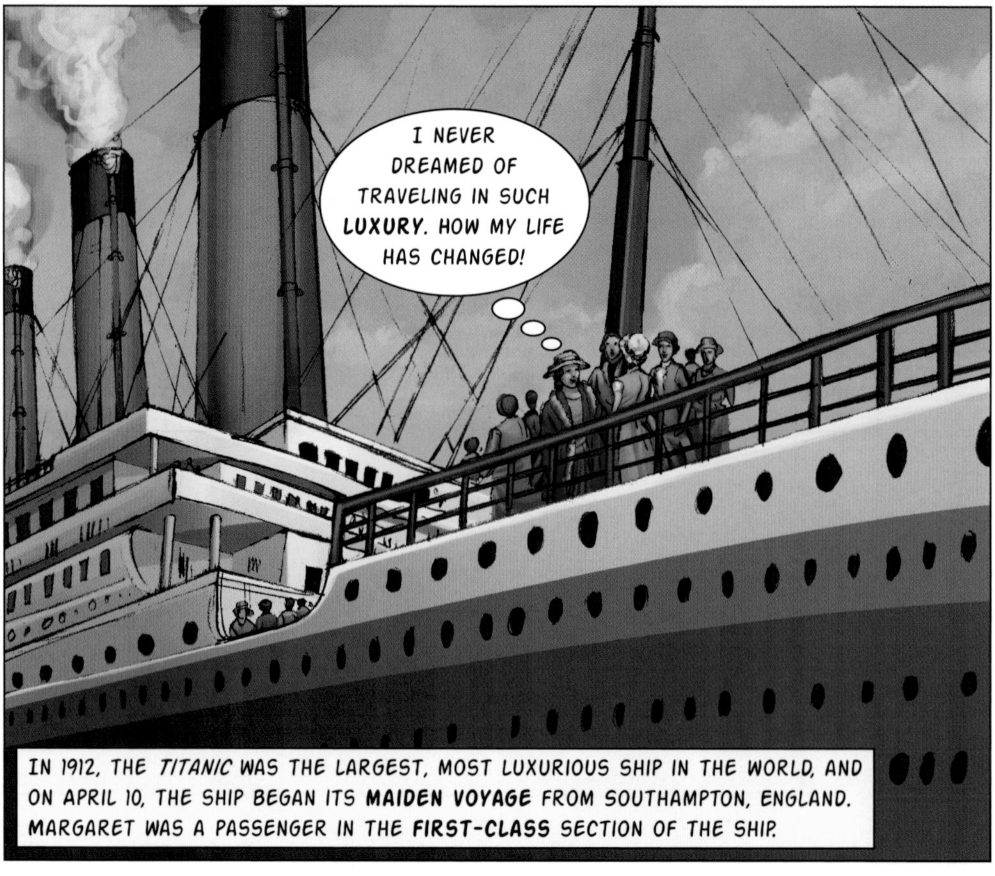
I NEVER DREAMED OF TRAVELING IN SUCH **LUXURY**. HOW MY LIFE HAS CHANGED!
IN 1912, THE *TITANIC* WAS THE LARGEST, MOST LUXURIOUS SHIP IN THE WORLD, AND ON APRIL 10, THE SHIP BEGAN ITS **MAIDEN VOYAGE** FROM SOUTHAMPTON, ENGLAND. MARGARET WAS A PASSENGER IN THE **FIRST-CLASS** SECTION OF THE SHIP.

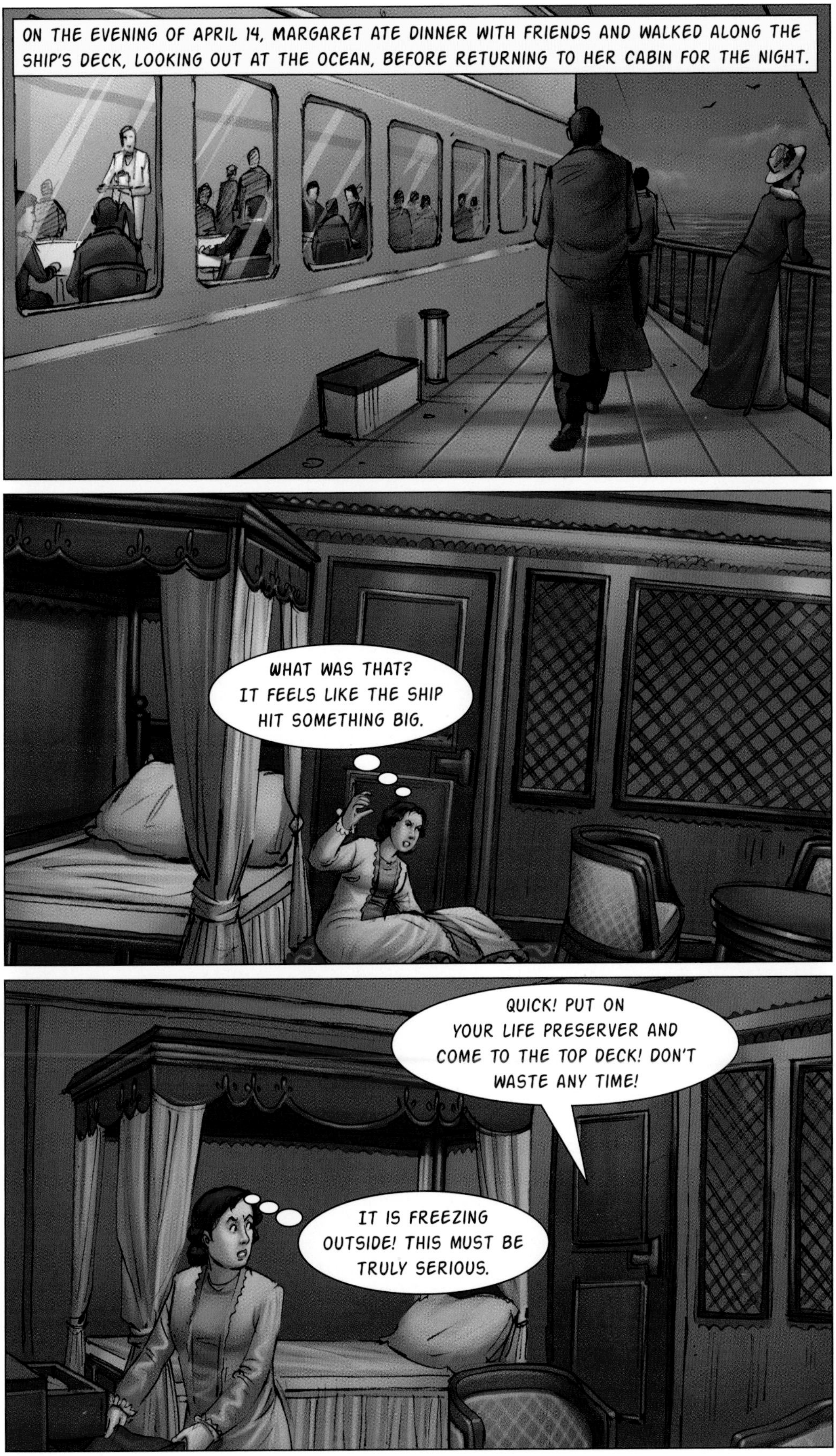
ON THE EVENING OF APRIL 14, MARGARET ATE DINNER WITH FRIENDS AND WALKED ALONG THE SHIP'S DECK, LOOKING OUT AT THE OCEAN, BEFORE RETURNING TO HER CABIN FOR THE NIGHT.
WHAT WAS THAT? IT FEELS LIKE THE SHIP HIT SOMETHING BIG.
QUICK! PUT ON YOUR LIFE PRESERVER AND COME TO THE TOP DECK! DON'T WASTE ANY TIME!
IT IS FREEZING OUTSIDE! THIS MUST BE TRULY SERIOUS.

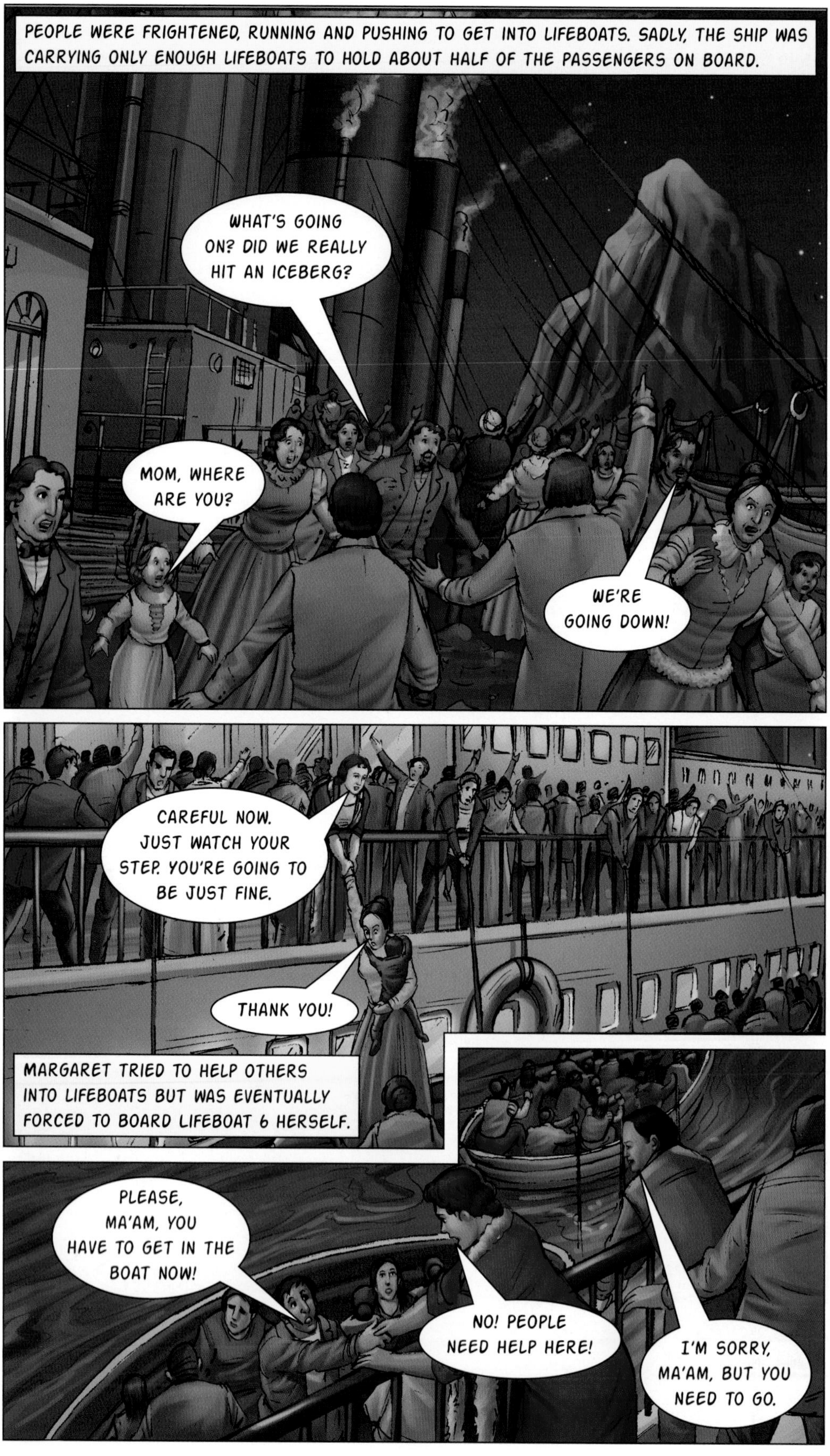
PEOPLE WERE FRIGHTENED, RUNNING AND PUSHING TO GET INTO LIFEBOATS. SADLY, THE SHIP WAS CARRYING ONLY ENOUGH LIFEBOATS TO HOLD ABOUT HALF OF THE PASSENGERS ON BOARD.
WHAT'S GOING ON? DID WE REALLY HIT AN ICEBERG?
MOM, WHERE ARE YOU?
WE'RE GOING DOWN!
CAREFUL NOW. JUST WATCH YOUR STEP. YOU'RE GOING TO BE JUST FINE.
THANK YOU!
MARGARET TRIED TO HELP OTHERS INTO LIFEBOATS BUT WAS EVENTUALLY FORCED TO BOARD LIFEBOAT 6 HERSELF.
PLEASE, MA'AM, YOU HAVE TO GET IN THE BOAT NOW!
NO! PEOPLE NEED HELP HERE!
I'M SORRY, MA'AM, BUT YOU NEED TO GO.

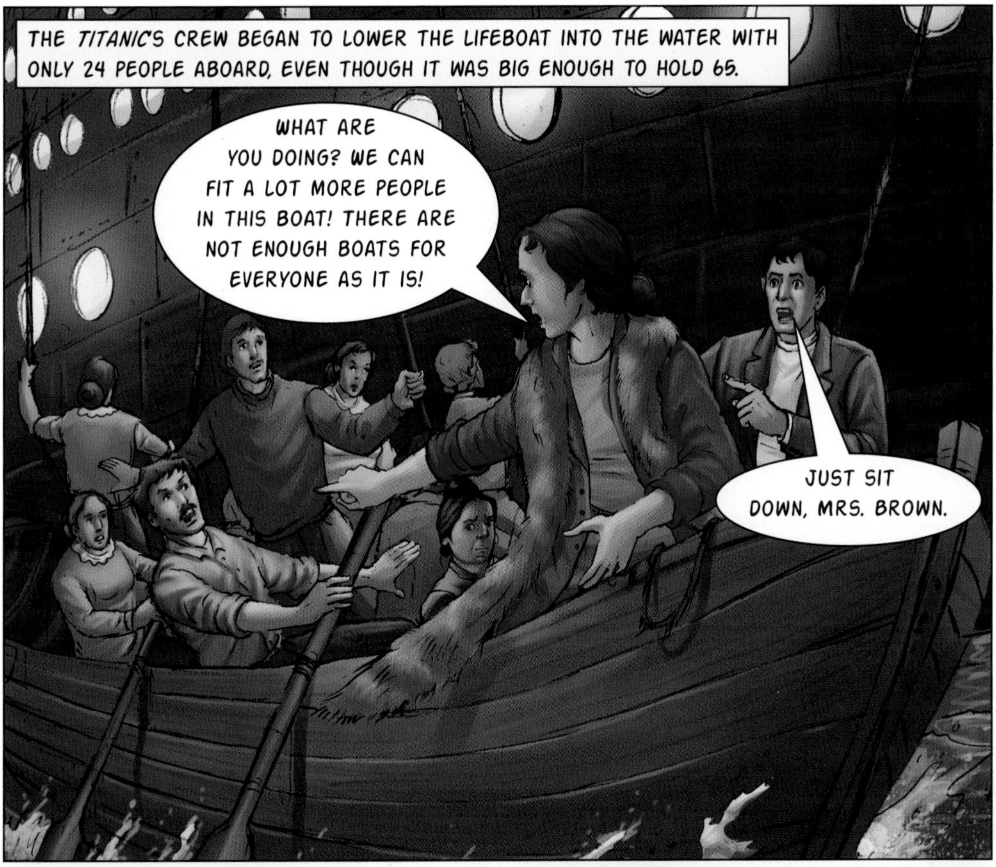
THE *TITANIC*'S CREW BEGAN TO LOWER THE LIFEBOAT INTO THE WATER WITH ONLY 24 PEOPLE ABOARD, EVEN THOUGH IT WAS BIG ENOUGH TO HOLD 65.
WHAT ARE YOU DOING? WE CAN FIT A LOT MORE PEOPLE IN THIS BOAT! THERE ARE NOT ENOUGH BOATS FOR EVERYONE AS IT IS!
JUST SIT DOWN, MRS. BROWN.

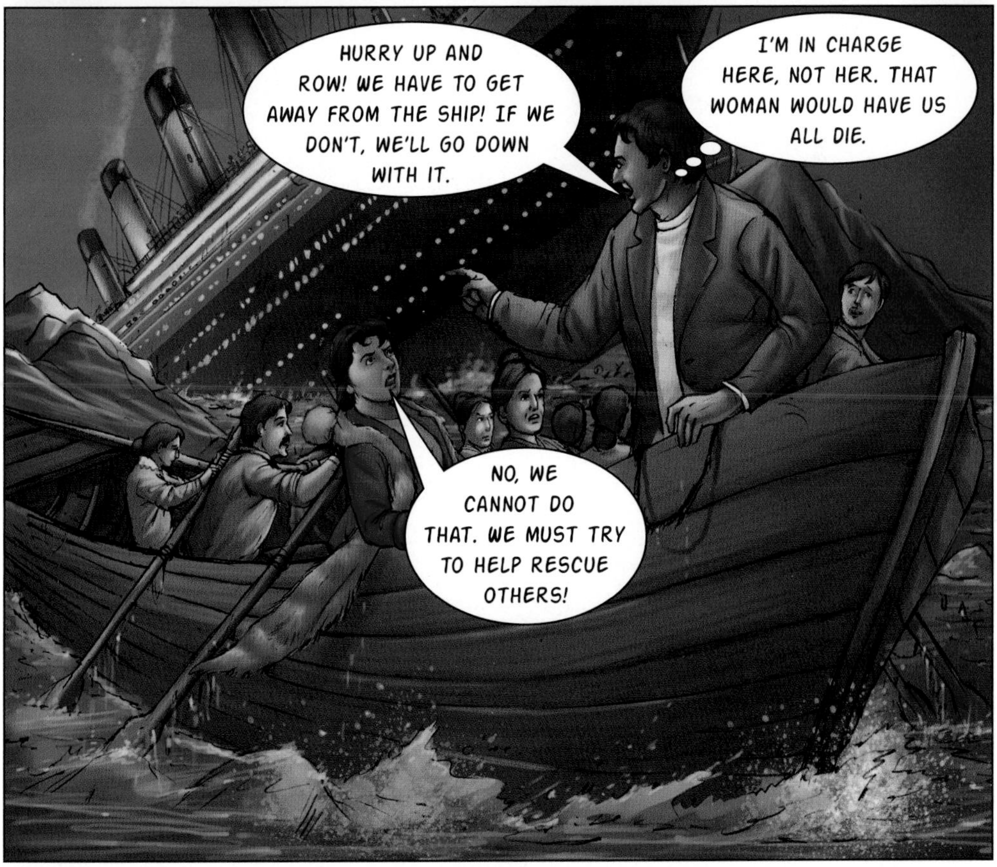
HURRY UP AND ROW! WE HAVE TO GET AWAY FROM THE SHIP! IF WE DON'T, WE'LL GO DOWN WITH IT.
I'M IN CHARGE HERE, NOT HER. THAT WOMAN WOULD HAVE US ALL DIE.
NO, WE CANNOT DO THAT. WE MUST TRY TO HELP RESCUE OTHERS!

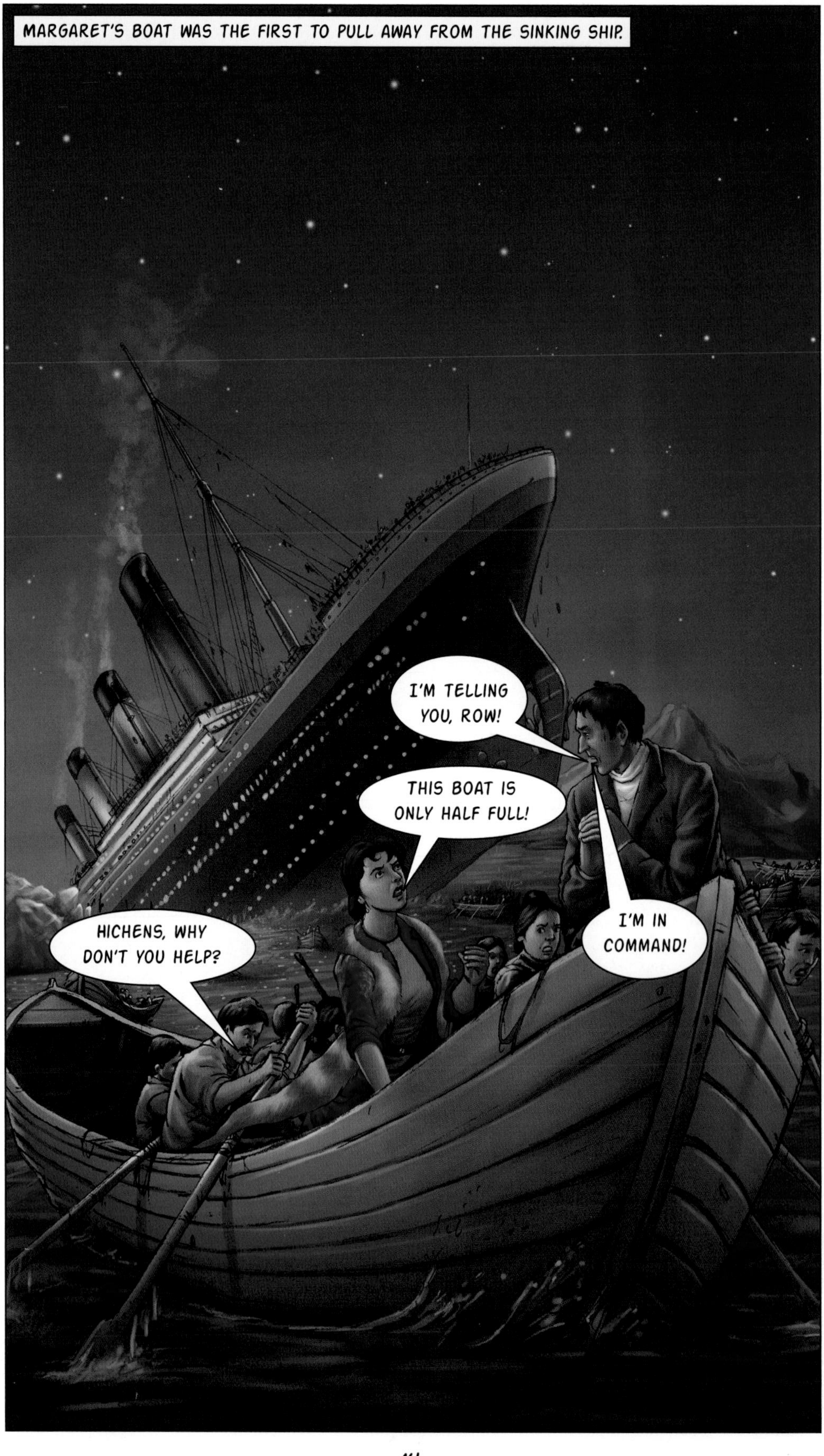
MARGARET'S BOAT WAS THE FIRST TO PULL AWAY FROM THE SINKING SHIP.
HICHENS, WHY DON'T YOU HELP?
THIS BOAT IS ONLY HALF FULL!
I'M TELLING YOU, ROW!
I'M IN COMMAND!

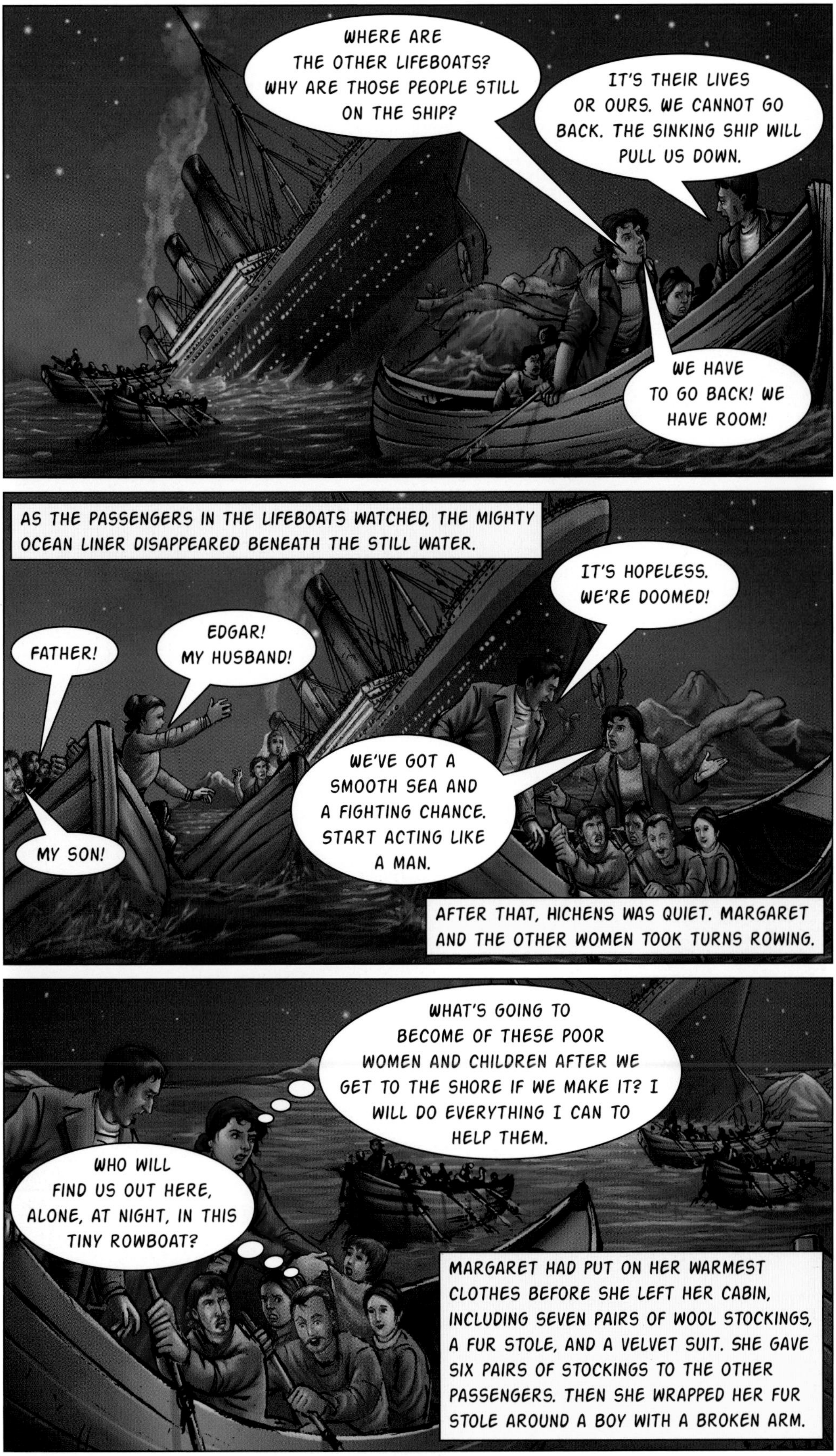
WHERE ARE THE OTHER LIFEBOATS? WHY ARE THOSE PEOPLE STILL ON THE SHIP?
IT'S THEIR LIVES OR OURS. WE CANNOT GO BACK. THE SINKING SHIP WILL PULL US DOWN.
WE HAVE TO GO BACK! WE HAVE ROOM!
AS THE PASSENGERS IN THE LIFEBOATS WATCHED, THE MIGHTY OCEAN LINER DISAPPEARED BENEATH THE STILL WATER.
FATHER!
EDGAR! MY HUSBAND!
IT'S HOPELESS. WE'RE DOOMED!
MY SON!
WE'VE GOT A SMOOTH SEA AND A FIGHTING CHANCE. START ACTING LIKE A MAN.
AFTER THAT, HICHENS WAS QUIET. MARGARET AND THE OTHER WOMEN TOOK TURNS ROWING.
WHAT'S GOING TO BECOME OF THESE POOR WOMEN AND CHILDREN AFTER WE GET TO THE SHORE IF WE MAKE IT? I WILL DO EVERYTHING I CAN TO HELP THEM.
WHO WILL FIND US OUT HERE, ALONE, AT NIGHT, IN THIS TINY ROWBOAT?
MARGARET HAD PUT ON HER WARMEST CLOTHES BEFORE SHE LEFT HER CABIN, INCLUDING SEVEN PAIRS OF WOOL STOCKINGS, A FUR STOLE, AND A VELVET SUIT. SHE GAVE SIX PAIRS OF STOCKINGS TO THE OTHER PASSENGERS. THEN SHE WRAPPED HER FUR STOLE AROUND A BOY WITH A BROKEN ARM.

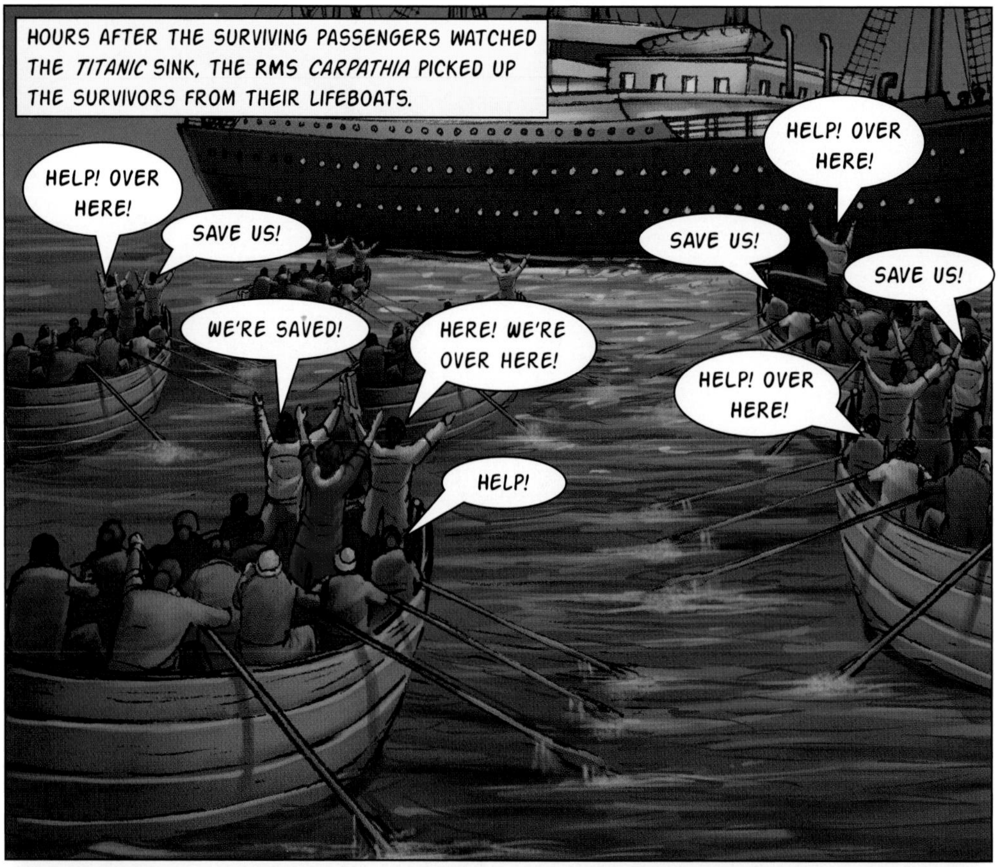
HOURS AFTER THE SURVIVING PASSENGERS WATCHED THE *TITANIC* SINK, THE RMS *CARPATHIA* PICKED UP THE SURVIVORS FROM THEIR LIFEBOATS.
HELP! OVER HERE!
SAVE US!
WE'RE SAVED!
HERE! WE'RE OVER HERE!
HELP!
HELP! OVER HERE!
SAVE US!
SAVE US!
HELP! OVER HERE!

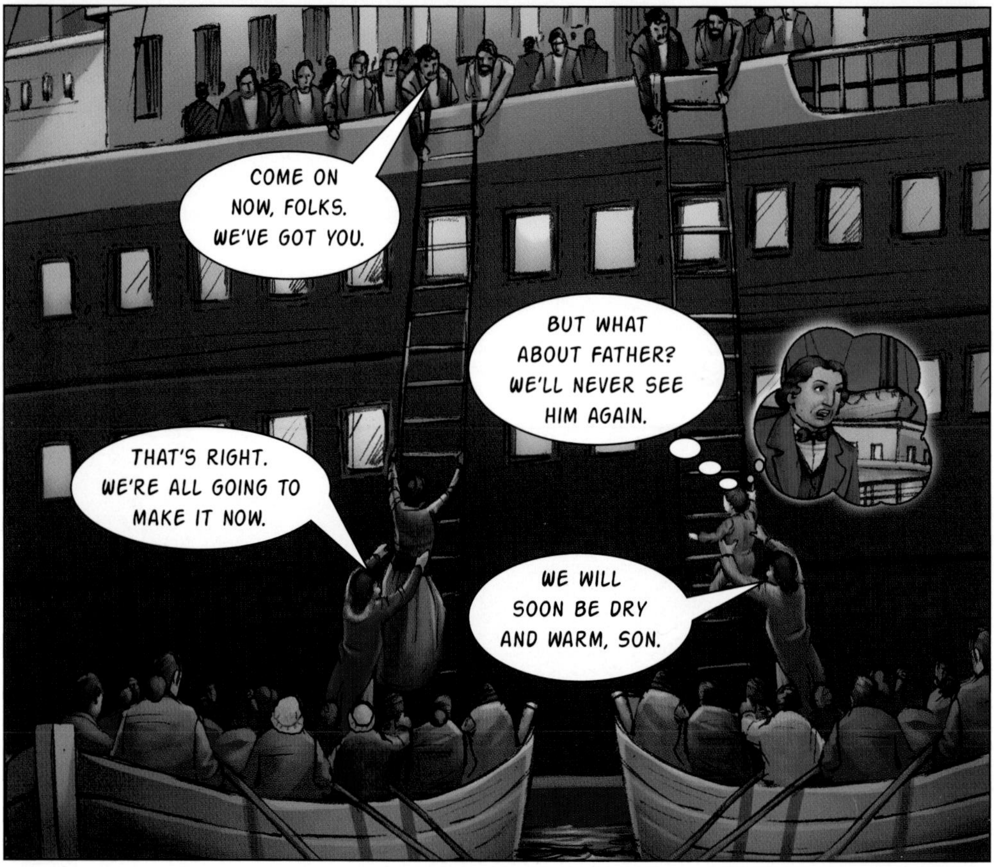
COME ON NOW, FOLKS. WE'VE GOT YOU.
THAT'S RIGHT. WE'RE ALL GOING TO MAKE IT NOW.
BUT WHAT ABOUT FATHER? WE'LL NEVER SEE HIM AGAIN.
WE WILL SOON BE DRY AND WARM, SON.

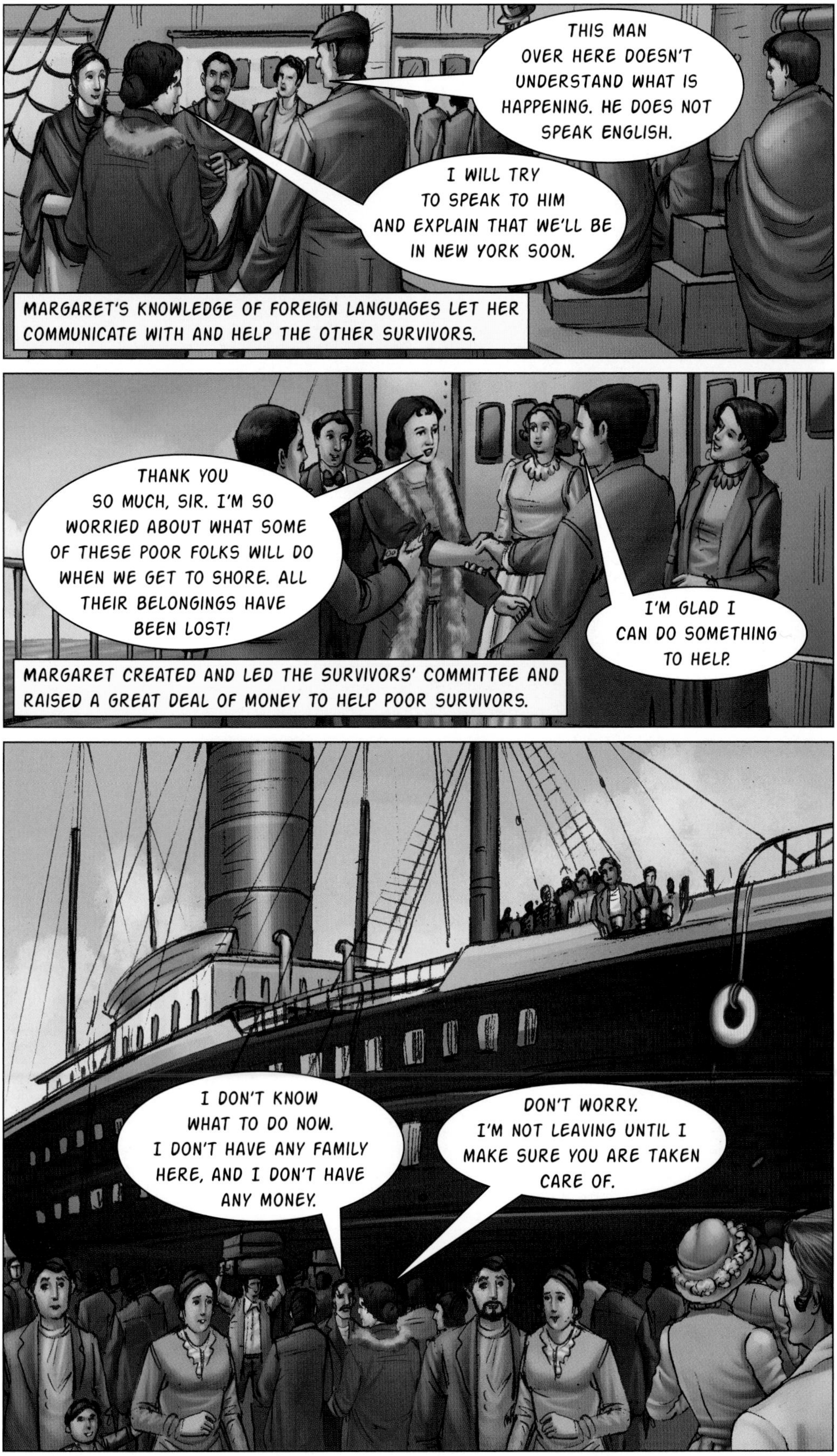
THIS MAN OVER HERE DOESN'T UNDERSTAND WHAT IS HAPPENING. HE DOES NOT SPEAK ENGLISH.
I WILL TRY TO SPEAK TO HIM AND EXPLAIN THAT WE'LL BE IN NEW YORK SOON.
MARGARET'S KNOWLEDGE OF FOREIGN LANGUAGES LET HER COMMUNICATE WITH AND HELP THE OTHER SURVIVORS.
THANK YOU SO MUCH, SIR. I'M SO WORRIED ABOUT WHAT SOME OF THESE POOR FOLKS WILL DO WHEN WE GET TO SHORE. ALL THEIR BELONGINGS HAVE BEEN LOST!
I'M GLAD I CAN DO SOMETHING TO HELP.
MARGARET CREATED AND LED THE SURVIVORS' COMMITTEE AND RAISED A GREAT DEAL OF MONEY TO HELP POOR SURVIVORS.
I DON'T KNOW WHAT TO DO NOW. I DON'T HAVE ANY FAMILY HERE, AND I DON'T HAVE ANY MONEY.
DON'T WORRY. I'M NOT LEAVING UNTIL I MAKE SURE YOU ARE TAKEN CARE OF.

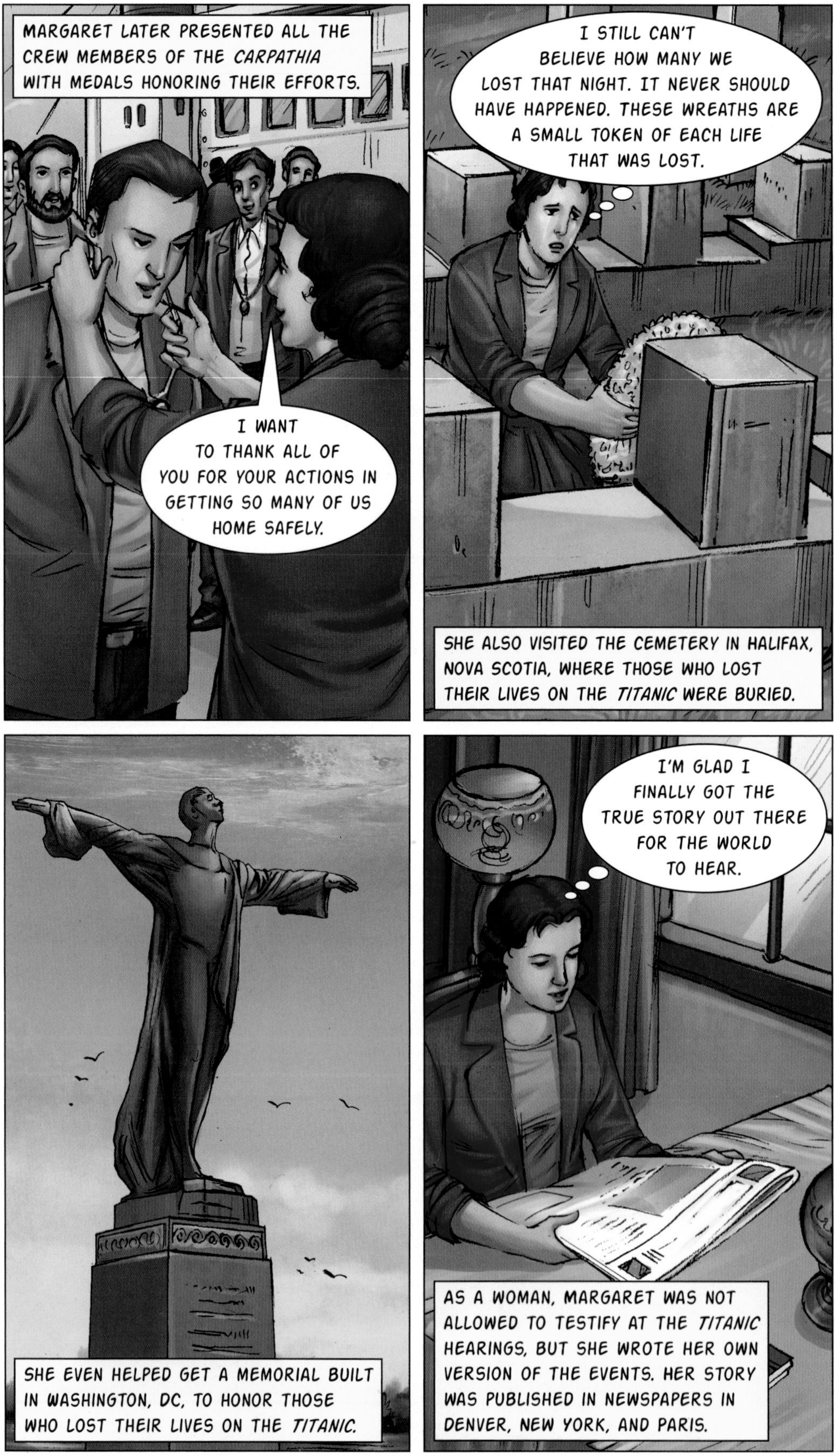
MARGARET LATER PRESENTED ALL THE CREW MEMBERS OF THE *CARPATHIA* WITH MEDALS HONORING THEIR EFFORTS.
I WANT TO THANK ALL OF YOU FOR YOUR ACTIONS IN GETTING SO MANY OF US HOME SAFELY.
I STILL CAN'T BELIEVE HOW MANY WE LOST THAT NIGHT. IT NEVER SHOULD HAVE HAPPENED. THESE WREATHS ARE A SMALL TOKEN OF EACH LIFE THAT WAS LOST.
SHE ALSO VISITED THE CEMETERY IN HALIFAX, NOVA SCOTIA, WHERE THOSE WHO LOST THEIR LIVES ON THE *TITANIC* WERE BURIED.
SHE EVEN HELPED GET A MEMORIAL BUILT IN WASHINGTON, DC, TO HONOR THOSE WHO LOST THEIR LIVES ON THE *TITANIC*.
I'M GLAD I FINALLY GOT THE TRUE STORY OUT THERE FOR THE WORLD TO HEAR.
AS A WOMAN, MARGARET WAS NOT ALLOWED TO TESTIFY AT THE *TITANIC* HEARINGS, BUT SHE WROTE HER OWN VERSION OF THE EVENTS. HER STORY WAS PUBLISHED IN NEWSPAPERS IN DENVER, NEW YORK, AND PARIS.

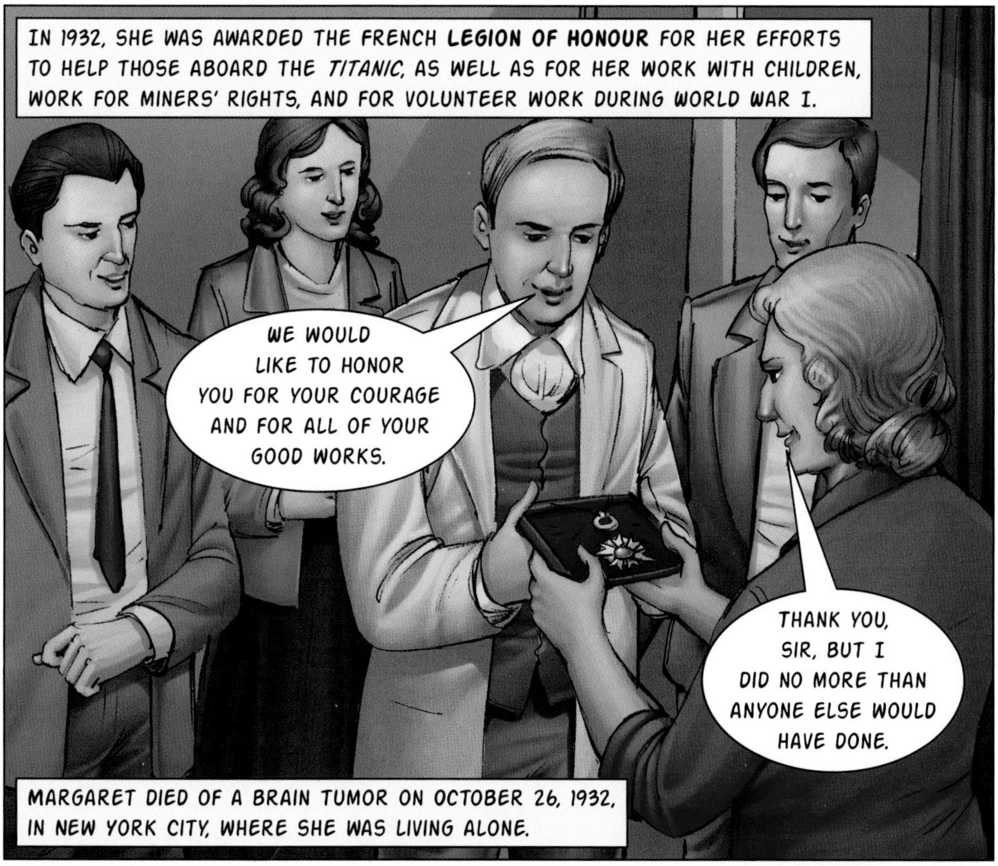
IN 1932, SHE WAS AWARDED THE FRENCH **LEGION OF HONOUR** FOR HER EFFORTS TO HELP THOSE ABOARD THE *TITANIC*, AS WELL AS FOR HER WORK WITH CHILDREN, WORK FOR MINERS' RIGHTS, AND FOR VOLUNTEER WORK DURING WORLD WAR I.
WE WOULD LIKE TO HONOR YOU FOR YOUR COURAGE AND FOR ALL OF YOUR GOOD WORKS.
THANK YOU, SIR, BUT I DID NO MORE THAN ANYONE ELSE WOULD HAVE DONE.
MARGARET DIED OF A BRAIN TUMOR ON OCTOBER 26, 1932, IN NEW YORK CITY, WHERE SHE WAS LIVING ALONE.

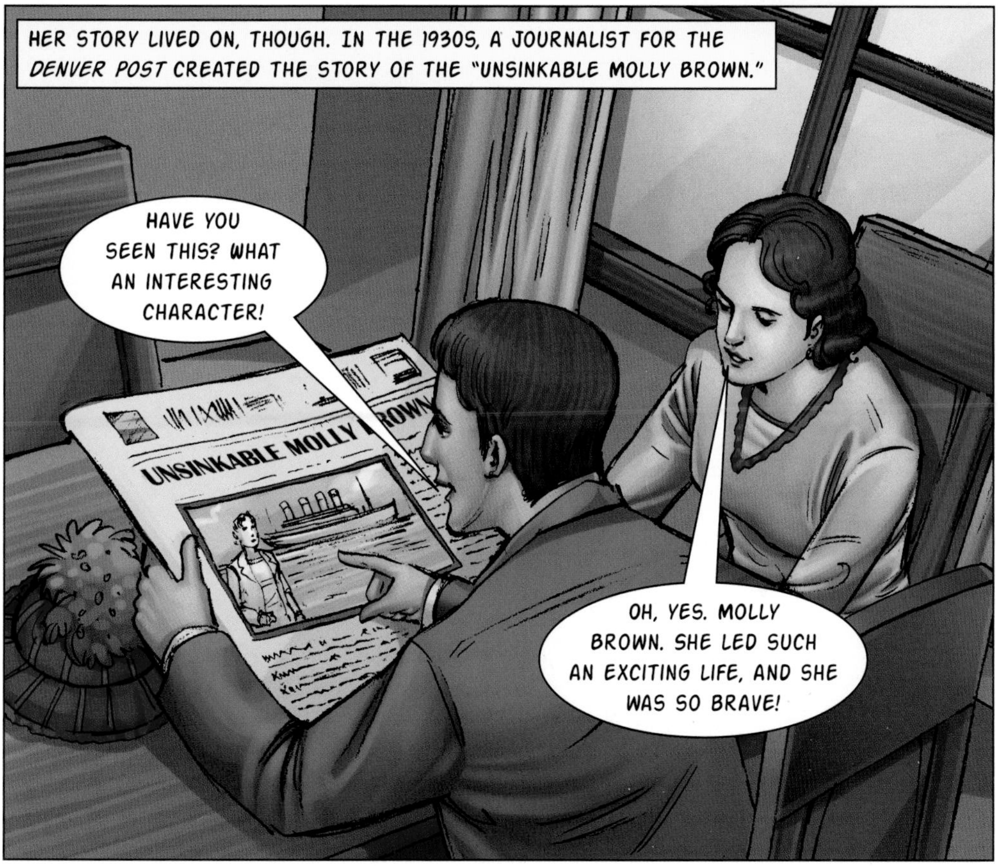
HER STORY LIVED ON, THOUGH. IN THE 1930S, A JOURNALIST FOR THE *DENVER POST* CREATED THE STORY OF THE "UNSINKABLE MOLLY BROWN."
HAVE YOU SEEN THIS? WHAT AN INTERESTING CHARACTER!
UNSINKABLE MOLLY BROWN
OH, YES. MOLLY BROWN. SHE LED SUCH AN EXCITING LIFE, AND SHE WAS SO BRAVE!

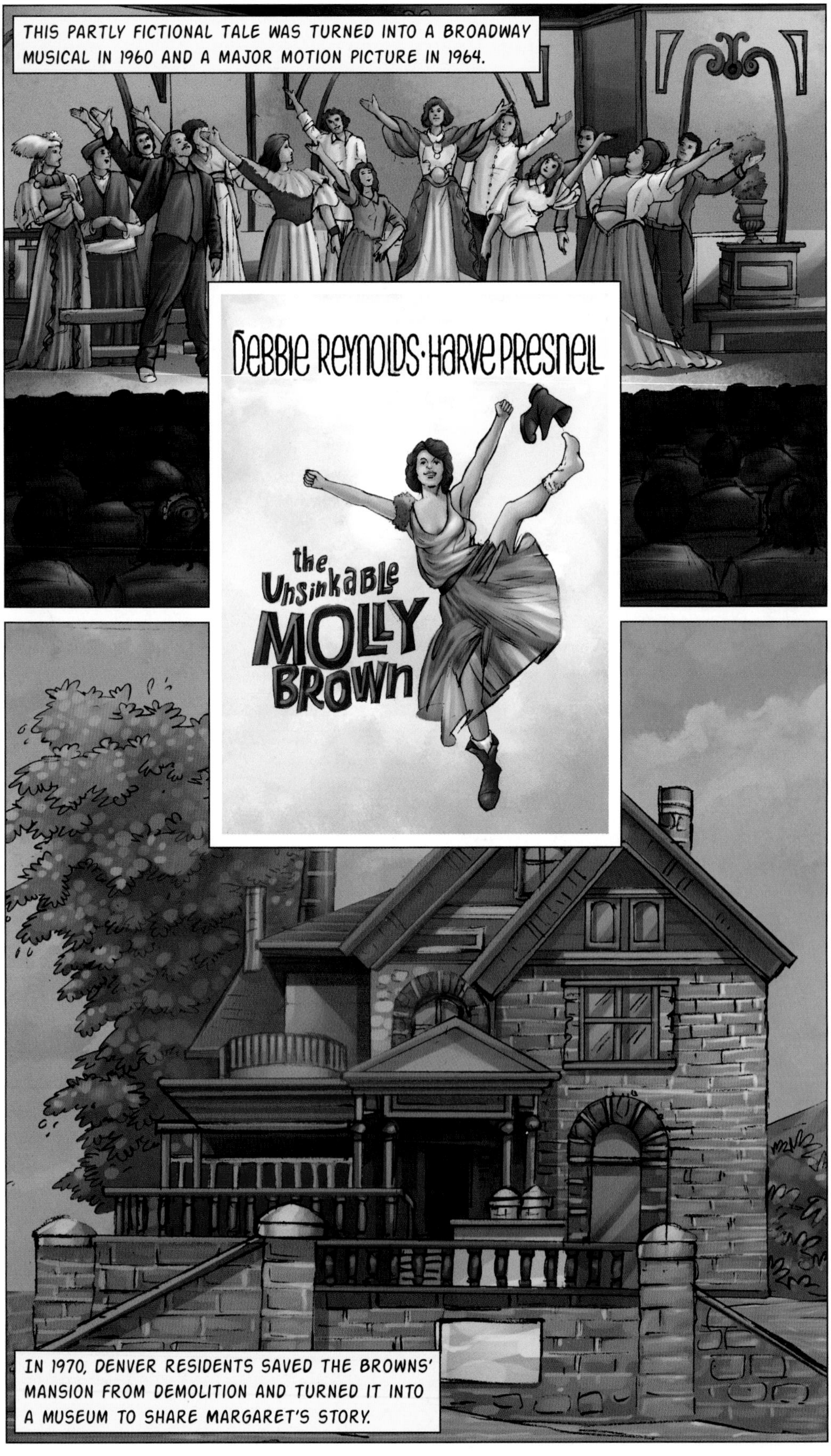
THIS PARTLY FICTIONAL TALE WAS TURNED INTO A BROADWAY MUSICAL IN 1960 AND A MAJOR MOTION PICTURE IN 1964.
DEBBIE REYNOLDS · HARVE PRESNELL
the Unsinkable MOLLY BROWN
IN 1970, DENVER RESIDENTS SAVED THE BROWNS' MANSION FROM DEMOLITION AND TURNED IT INTO A MUSEUM TO SHARE MARGARET'S STORY.

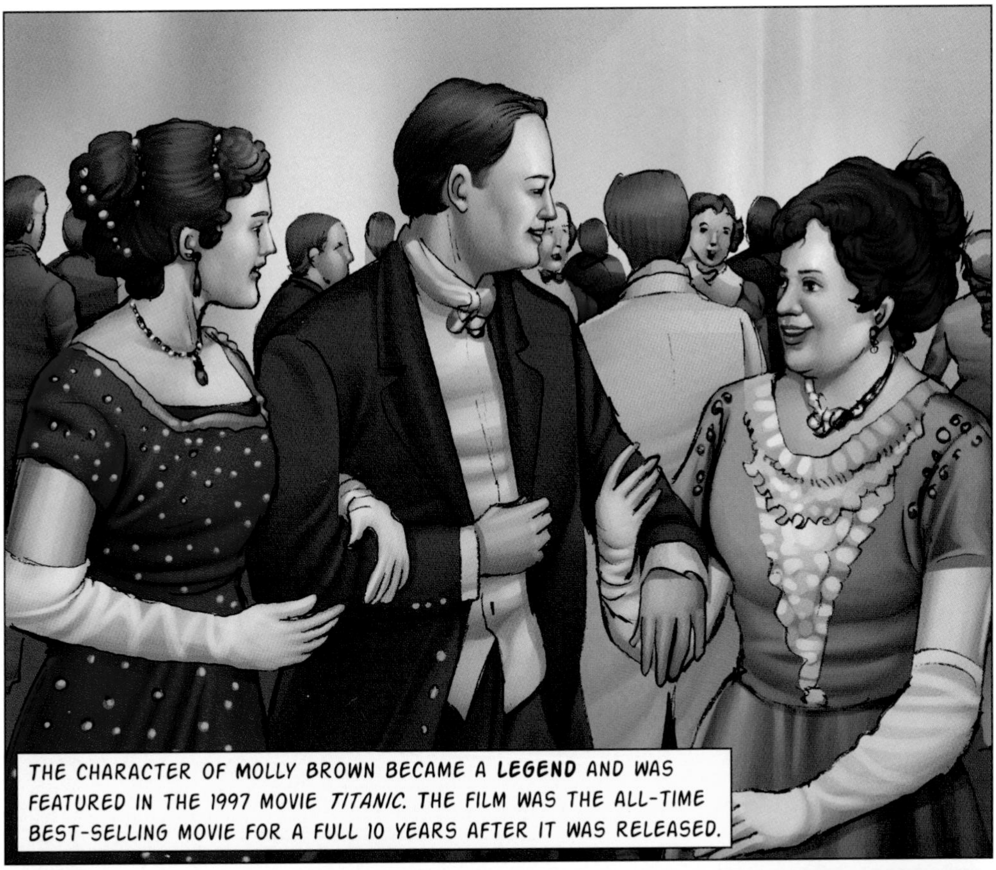
THE CHARACTER OF MOLLY BROWN BECAME A **LEGEND** AND WAS FEATURED IN THE 1997 MOVIE *TITANIC*. THE FILM WAS THE ALL-TIME BEST-SELLING MOVIE FOR A FULL 10 YEARS AFTER IT WAS RELEASED.

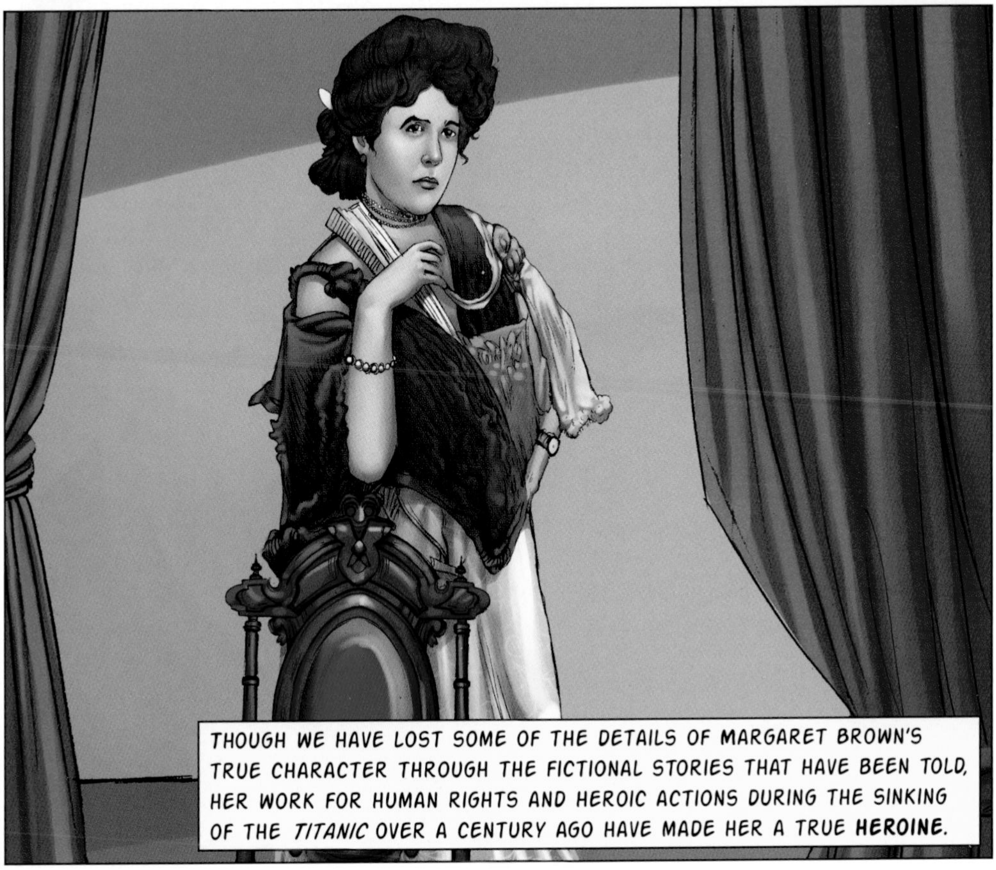
THOUGH WE HAVE LOST SOME OF THE DETAILS OF MARGARET BROWN'S TRUE CHARACTER THROUGH THE FICTIONAL STORIES THAT HAVE BEEN TOLD, HER WORK FOR HUMAN RIGHTS AND HEROIC ACTIONS DURING THE SINKING OF THE *TITANIC* OVER A CENTURY AGO HAVE MADE HER A TRUE **HEROINE**.

Timeline

July 18, 1867	Margaret Tobin is born in Hannibal, Missouri.
1886	Margaret moves to Leadville, Colorado, with her brother.
September 1886	Margaret marries James Joseph Brown.
1887	Margaret gives birth to her first child, Lawrence Palmer.
1889	Margaret's second child, Catherine Ellen, called Helen, is born.
1893	Margaret's work for the women's suffrage movement helps get women the vote in Colorado.
1894	After becoming wealthy, the Brown family moves to a mansion in Denver.
1901	Margaret studies at the Carnegie Institute.
1909	Margaret and J. J. separate.
April 10, 1912	Margaret leaves Europe for New York on the RMS *Titanic*.
April 14, 1912	The *Titanic* hits an iceberg and, on April 15, the ship sinks. Margaret's actions help survivors.
1932	Margaret is awarded the French Legion of Honour.
October 26, 1932	Margaret dies of a brain tumor.
November 30, 1960	The musical *The Unsinkable Molly Brown* opens on Broadway.
1964	The film adaption of the musical is released.

Glossary

disaster (dih-ZAS-ter) An event that causes suffering or loss.

draperies (DRAY-puh-reez) Decorative material that is hung around windows.

engineer (en-juh-NEER) A master at planning and building engines, machines, roads, mines, and bridges.

first-class (FURST-KLAS) The highest quality.

heroine (HER-uh-wun) A woman or girl who is brave, does good things, and has a noble character.

immigrants (IH-muh-grunts) People who move to a new country from another country.

legend (LEH-jend) A person who has been famous and honored for a very long time.

Legion of Honour (LEE-jen UV ON-er) The highest honor given in France; it is awarded for high achievement.

lifeboats (LYF-bohts) Small, sturdy boats carried by larger boats for use in emergencies.

luxury (LUK-shuh-ree) Comforts and beauties of life that are not necessary.

maiden voyage (MAY-den VOY-ij) A ship's first journey at sea.

mercantile store (MER-kun-teel STOR) A place where many different kinds of goods were sold.

Sherman Silver Purchase Act (SHER-mun SIL-ver PUR-chus AKT) A law passed in 1890 that required the US government to increase greatly the amount of silver it purchased.

suffrage (SUH-frij) The right of voting.

superintendent (soo-prin-TEN-dent) Someone who oversees others' work.

voyage (VOY-ij) A journey, especially by water.

Index

WebSites

Due to the changing nature of Internet links, PowerKids Press has developed an online list of websites related to the subject of this book. This site is updated regularly. Please use this link to access the link:

www.powerkidslinks.com/jgam/brown/